*Gre؟
in Ebook and Audiobook format.

Greater Than a Tourist Book Series
Reviews from Readers

I think the series is wonderful and beneficial for tourists to get information before visiting the city.

-Seckin Zumbul, Izmir Turkey

I am a world traveler who has read many trip guides but this one really made a difference for me. I would call it a heartfelt creation of a local guide expert instead of just a guide.

-Susy, Isla Holbox, Mexico

New to the area like me, this is a must have!

-Joe, Bloomington, USA

This is a good series that gets down to it when looking for things to do at your destination without having to read a novel for just a few ideas.

-Rachel, Monterey, USA

Good information to have to plan my trip to this destination.

-Pennie Farrell, Mexico

Great ideas for a port day.

-Mary Martin USA

Aptly titled, you won't just be a tourist after reading this book. You'll be greater than a tourist!

-Alan Warner, Grand Rapids, USA

Even though I only have three days to spend in San Miguel in an upcoming visit, I will use the author's suggestions to guide some of my time there. An easy read - with chapters named to guide me in directions I want to go.

 -Robert Catapano, USA

Great insights from a local perspective! Useful information and a very good value!

 -Sarah, USA

This series provides an in-depth experience through the eyes of a local. Reading these series will help you to travel the city in with confidence and it'll make your journey a unique one.

-Andrew Teoh, Ipoh, Malaysia

GREATER THAN A TOURIST- NASSAU NEW PROVIDENCE BAHAMAS

50 Travel Tips from a Local

Aradhana Gilbert

CZYK
PUBLISHING

CZYK Publishing Since 2011.
Greater Than a Tourist

Lock Haven, PA
All rights reserved.

ISBN: 9798633383164

>TOURIST

50 TRAVEL TIPS FROM A LOCAL

BOOK DESCRIPTION

With travel tips and culture in our guidebooks written by a local author, it is never too late to visit Nassau. Greater Than a Tourist- Nassau, Bahamas by Author Aradhana Gilbert offers the inside scoop on the hottest Caribbean summer destination, The Bahamas. Most travel books tell you how to travel like a tourist. Although there is nothing wrong with that, as part of the 'Greater Than a Tourist' series, this book will give you candid travel tips from someone who has lived at your next travel destination. This guide book will not tell you exact addresses or store hours but instead gives you knowledge that you may not find in other smaller print travel books. Experience cultural, culinary delights, and attractions with the guidance of a Local. Slow down and get to know the people with this invaluable guide. By the time you finish this book, you will be eager and prepared to discover new activities at your next travel destination.

Inside this travel guide book you will find:

Visitor information from a Local
Tour ideas and inspiration
Save time with valuable guidebook information

Greater Than a Tourist- A Travel Guidebook with 50 Travel Tips from a Local. Slow down, stay in one place, and get to know the people and culture. By the time you finish this book, you will be eager and prepared to travel to your next destination.

OUR STORY

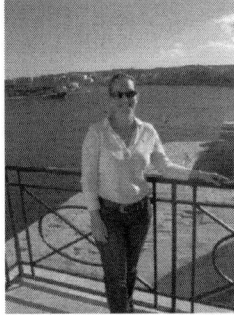

Traveling is a passion of the Greater than a Tourist book series creator. Lisa studied abroad in college, and for their honeymoon Lisa and her husband toured Europe. During her travels to Malta, an older man tried to give her some advice based on his own experience living on the island since he was a young boy. She was not sure if she should talk to the stranger but was interested in his advice. When traveling to some places she was wary to talk to locals because she was afraid that they weren't being genuine. Through her travels, Lisa learned how much locals had to share with tourists. Lisa created the Greater Than a Tourist book series to help connect people with locals. A topic that locals are very passionate about sharing.

TABLE OF CONTENTS

14. Carnival is in Trinidad, Junkanoo is in The Bahamas
15. Bonfire on the Beach
16. Ardastra Gardens, Zoo and Conservation Center is the Bahamian Version of a Zoo and Botanical Garden
17. Feeding Needs of Your Infants
18. Clothing Needs for Your Children
19. Clothing Needs for Yourself
20. The Bahamas is an Environmentally Friendly Country
21. Leave No Trace (Trash or Markings)
22. How to See the Whole Island
23. Charter a Boat or Yacht for Fishing or Sailing
24. Are all Beaches for the Public
25. You can Travel to the Out Islands/Family Islands
26. Most Surprising Rock Shore
27. Food Prices and VAT
28. Rose Island Day Trip
29. Waterproof Camera
30. Bahamas Kayaking and Water Sports Package at Junkanoo Beach
31. Nassau Food Tasting and Cultural Walking Tour
32. Nassau Submarine Adventure
33. Exuma Adventures

DEDICATION

This book is dedicated to my nephew, Asher. Always take opportunities to travel and explore new places. I look forward to traveling with you.

To Mom, Sister, Brother-in-law, Sister's future kids, and extended family.

For the people who dream of travel, and for the people who travel.

ABOUT THE AUTHOR

Aradhana is a daughter and sister who is a native of The Bahamas. She loves to spend endless hours exploring her country and playing with her nephew.

HOW TO USE THIS BOOK

The *Greater Than a Tourist* book series was written by someone who has lived in an area for over three months. The goal of this book is to help travelers either dream or experience different locations by providing opinions from a local. The author has made suggestions based on their own experiences. Please check before traveling to the area in case the suggested places are unavailable.

Travel Advisories: As a first step in planning any trip abroad, check the Travel Advisories for your intended destination.
https://travel.state.gov/content/travel/en/traveladvisories/traveladvisories.html

FROM THE PUBLISHER

Traveling can be one of the most important parts of a person's life. The anticipation and memories that you have are some of the best. As a publisher of the Greater Than a Tourist, as well as the popular *50 Things to Know* book series, we strive to help you learn about new places, spark your imagination, and inspire you. Wherever you are and whatever you do I wish you safe, fun, and inspiring travel.

Lisa Rusczyk Ed. D.
CZYK Publishing

WELCOME TO
> TOURIST

Astronaut Photo of Nassau, The Bahamas taken from the International Space Station (ISS) during Expedition 22 on January 1, 2010

Parliament of the Bahamas, located in downtown Nassau, is the meeting place of the two houses of the Bahamian Parliament.

Aerial view of the Hilton resort in Nassau

A panoramic view of Prince George Wharf, the facility serving passenger cruise ships in Nassau Harbour, off the island of New Providence in the Bahamas. Seen docked along the wharf, left to right, are the MS Carnival Fascination, MS Disney Wonder, MS Carnival Sensation, and Royal Caribbean International's MS Majesty Of The Seas.

*"Life is either a daring
adventure or nothing at all."*

-Helen Keller

    This brief guide is a compilation of important information and tips that every Tourist to The Bahamas should have at his/her fingertips. I hope that readers will find the information to be both useful and interesting. Happy travels!

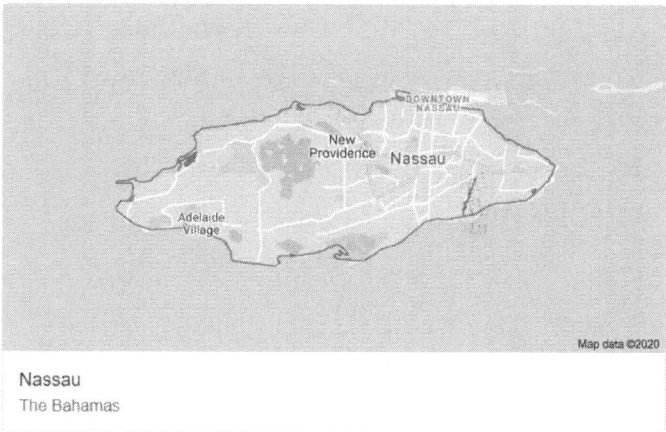

Nassau
The Bahamas

Nassau Climate

	High	Low
January	79	64
February	79	64
March	81	65
April	83	68
May	86	71
June	89	74
July	90	76
August	91	76
September	90	75
October	87	73
November	83	69
December	80	66

GreaterThanaTourist.com

Temperatures are in Fahrenheit degrees.
Source: NOAA

1. CURRENCY TO CARRY

In the Bahamas, the accepted currencies are the Bahamian dollar (BSD) and the United States dollar (USD). There will always be an ATM within walking distance of a tourist attraction or a beach. Visa, Mastercard, and most debit cards are also widely accepted. Some banks may charge international transaction fees. You should consult with your provider before leaving home.

Traveling tip: Consider upgrading to a travel credit card. Depending on your bank, you can initiate money transfers in BSD or USD currencies and get notifications about any activity in real-time. A travel credit card makes it easier to access funds while traveling. You will avoid paying some international transaction fees.

2. GREETING THE LOCALS

In the Bahamas, many of the citizens speak English. When initiating conservation with a local, it is considered polite to smile and greet them. Greetings commonly accepted in the English language are accepted here. You can say 'Good day' regardless of what time it is. Bahamians also engage in Bahamian dialect which may differ slightly from island to island.

3. DRESS CODES, DRESS CODES, DRESS CODES

Tourists usually dress to their level of comfort and if you feel happy in what you are wearing, Bahamians will accept you with open arms. The country has no dress codes. You can wear a bikini on the beach and through the streets of downtown. Summer brings humidity and heat. Be sure to pack shorts, sunblock, and bring a reusable water bottle. Winter nights are comfortably cool; however, you should have a light jacket or windbreaker should you hope to go out for a night on the town.

Travel tip: Some restaurants may have dress codes. Be sure to call ahead or carry an extra set of semi-casual or formal clothes on hand.

4. BEST PLACE TO FIND A TAXI OR RENTAL CAR OR RIDE SERVICE

When you walk out of the airport, there will be taxis situated outside willing to assist you. You can expect to find taxis near every tourist attraction. The hotel can call and arrange a personal taxi service for you during your stay. Many visitors arrange their rides using Airbnb's 'Ride Service Experience' that are given by locals in their car.

Book your rental car online three months before your trip. Make sure to call ahead to confirm. You will have to get a taxi for a ride over to the rental car location if you have luggage; however, if you are traveling light you can take a brisk walk over to rental car center that is at the airport.

Travel tip: Remember to call the hotel and to find out if they offer a shuttle service from the airport. Renting a car for the duration of your trip is a cheaper option than traveling via taxis.

5. BEST TIME TO TRAVEL

Year-round warm climate makes any season of the year the ideal time to travel. The list of year-round activities is endless due to Tourism being the number one industry.

The Bahamas is a great beach destination. There are so many water activities that you can take part in. People come to swim with the dolphins, to scuba dive, explore our blue hole, parasailing, snorkeling, fishing, sailing and so much more.

Travel tip: Book your trip by February to grab the best deals. In my experience, prices tend to hike up closer to the summer due to the demand.

The tragedy that struck the Bahamian island, Abaco, in 2019 was Hurricane Dorian. The Atlantic hurricane season is from June 1 to November 30. In the Bahamas, the peak period for Hurricanes are usually August to October. Hurricane occurrences are not frequent in The Bahamas, but they do happen. Research and plan before booking your trip. The maximum hurricane wind speed for the Bahamas was recorded as 185 mph. All flights, cruise ships, and boat excursions are cancelled when there's a hurricane warning.

Travel tip: Always add traveler's insurance to your trip if you are planning on visiting during Hurricane Season. If you are planning on visiting during Hurricane Season and have no prior hurricane experience, do not book an Airbnb but try to book a hotel or resort. During a hurricane, the hotel will provide you with amenities to make your stay comfortable. The hotel's generators are powered to last for the days, there most likely will be Wi-Fi, complimentary snacks, and 24/7 service.

If you have an Airbnb, you'll be either advised by the Host to move to the hotel, shelter or even stay in the Airbnb during the hurricane. Hurricane proofing a home takes time, skill, and effort. You will have to secure hurricane shutters, pack up all lawn decorations and equipment, buy survival supplies like flashlights, batteries, and canned food. You can view any of the hurricane preparedness checklist online posted by the Bahamian government, U.S Embassy in the Bahamas, or the American Red Cross. The taxis and bus system will most likely not be in operation during a Hurricane alert.

6. PLACES TO STAY

I would 100% recommend staying in a hotel rather than an Airbnb because they are centrally located near tourist attractions, beaches, and hot vacation spots. The hotels have better access to casinos, pools, water parks, and high-end dining experiences. Some of your meals are included depending on your hotel's vacation package. However, if you are traveling with low budget carefully select your Airbnb location that is at least near to a bus stop to avoid comparably high taxi fares.

Travel tip: Some hotels offer discounts to adventure experiences like Scooba diving, hiking, and local tours. Always do your research before committing to a place.

7. BEST PLACES FOR DINNER

The best dinner spot for an authentic Bahamian diner is at 'Fish Fry' (also known as 'Arawak Cay'). The 'Fish Fry' is located twenty minutes away from central Downtown by walking. The route from Downtown to 'Fish Fry' is walk-friendly. Some restaurants I frequently dine at are the 'Twin Brothers', 'Big Yard Fish Fry' and 'Frankie Gone Bananas'. Most of the restaurants at Arawak Cay have outdoor seating.

There are amazing fine dining options at Baha-mar and Atlantis. You can visit Yelp, TripAdvisor, or Airbnb to see new upcoming restaurants and promotions.

Travel tip: If you do not have a data plan yet, you can use your hotel's or ship's Wi-Fi to load your intended location into Google maps. Test it out in your home country so you can master it beforehand.

8. SIMPLE HACKS FOR TRAVELING WITH CHILDREN

If you are traveling with children, make sure to keep them hydrated by packing water bottles everywhere you go.

Some visitors find Bahamian food to be a little bit spicy, make sure to ask the server about the spice level.

The best souvenir shop for kids to find a special memento of their vacation is the local Straw Market.

It is home to handmade Bahamian crafts, gifts, and souvenirs.

Bring games to keep your kids occupied on the airplane. Bring coloring books, travel-size puzzles, and pre-load games on your electrical devices.

Arawak Cay has a restaurant called 'Twin Brothers'. There are known for the best daiquiri on the island. Bahamian Daiquiris comes in many popular flavors such as Mango, Miami vice, Strawberry and Pina colada.

9. ALWAYS BRING SUN BLOCK

Sunblock is somewhat expensive in the Bahamas. Bring your favorite bottle with you especially if you plan on getting a tan. Reapply even when you don't feel the need to. Your skin will thank you for it later. If you forget your sunblock lotion, just ask your taxi to point you in the direction of a pharmacy or food store to easily obtain some.

Travel tip: If you are planning on getting a tan, a good rule to follow is to always move your body for even coverage and make sure to set a timer to reapply sunscreen as directed by your bottle's instructions.

10. ALCOHOL: RULES, LAWS, AND TWEAKING YOUR DRINK

The legal drinking age in The Bahamas is 18. Alcohol is sold in liquor stores and most restaurants. It is available for consumption every day; however, you will be asked for your ID if you look under the legal drinking age. Alcohol and especially beer are cheaper in the Bahamas than it is in the United States. Some restaurants might have a Bahamian twist on your usual drink order, make sure to try it, and leave a review on that restaurant's page.

Beers to Try:

A popular local beer marked as being 'The Beer of the Bahamas' is Kalik, produced by Commonwealth Brewery. The Bahamian Brewery are the makers of Sands, Sands Light, Strong Back Stout, High Rock Lager and Bush Crack Beer.

You can call ahead to a brewery to schedule a tour. You will be required to bring your ID. You will be able to taste test the beers and decide for yourself which beer option you'd want to bring back home with you.

Travel tip: You can bring back two liters of alcohol duty-free, if one is locally produced. Make sure to keep your receipts to present it at the airport's check-in gate and to the customs officer in your country.

11. LIFEGUARDS MIGHT NOT BE ON DUTY

Many of my foreign friends are shocked to find that some of the Bahamian beaches don't have an active lifeguard on duty. Research and find out which beaches do and do not have a lifeguard on duty. If you are traveling with kids that need extra supervision, I would recommend a hotel that's situated right on the beach because they are guaranteed to have lifeguards. Some examples of hotels with an active lifeguard are Atlantis, Ocean Club, Sandals, and Baha-Mar.

Travel tip: Always keep an eye on your kids and know their specific location especially when they are in the pool or in the ocean.

12. CAKE BY THE OCEAN

Try the Rum Cake

Rum Cake is yellow cake infused with rum. Trust me and try the Bahamian rum cake. You won't regret it.

Take your significant other out for a picnic on the beach to watch the sunrise over the ocean. Get your Instagram 'couple goals' picture and bask in the golden rays. Aim to get this done on the first and last day you are on the beach. You can compare the before and after photos of your glowing tan and stress-free face.

Travel tip: At the airport, before you leave you can buy and take it to your home country. It will be duty-free.

13. DON'T ORDER PEPSI OR COKE, ORDER GOOMBAY PUNCH INSTEAD

Goombay Punch is a pineapple soda made only in the Bahamas. You can ask your bartender for the Goombay Smash (Goombay Punch & Rum) or look at the menu to see if the bar has something similar on their menu.

Travel tip: You can buy this at the airport to take home with you. It will be duty-free.

14. CARNIVAL IS IN TRINIDAD, JUNKANOO IS IN THE BAHAMAS

I find that foreigners are more familiar with the Carnival festival than with Junkanoo. Junkanoo is a parade celebrated on Boxing Day, the day after Christmas, showcasing Bahamian culture. There will be costumes, cowbells, horns, drums, singing, and dancing. If you miss it on Boxing Day, you can still catch the Junkanoo New Year's Day Parade and there is even Junkanoo in June.

I find that the noteworthy difference between the two festivals is in the audience's active participation. In Carnival, people are encouraged to participate by buying their costumes and join in with the dancing festivities. Junkanoo is a talent competition between the different parading groups. Junkanoo groups create their costumes, rehearse band music, and choreograph their moves. With Junkanoo, you can expect metal benches or standing room only areas to observe the parade.

Travel tip: Bring your drink to the festival to avoid walking a long distance to get refreshments. Always leave earlier to avoid traffic jams. Junkanoo parade tickets are usually purchased in advance if you would like to sit and observe the parade. Details are usually posted on the Ministry of Tourism website.

15. BONFIRE ON THE BEACH

'Bonfire on the Beach' is a night activity tour that's best done in a group. I had the opportunity to go on a tour to the 'Pirates of the Bahamas Beach Theme Park' which includes dancing, dinner, and a beach bonfire. You can take your kids on this tour. You will learn some Bahamian quick step dances that will impress your friends back at home.

The tour guides were friendly, and they will drop you back to the pickup location. The only con to this tour is that you must wait until the tour guides are ready to drop you back. I would suggest arranging a ride service if you plan on doing an activity proceeding the tour.

I did the tour by myself and I honestly was not expecting to enjoy it, but it was a pleasant surprise. I would not recommend doing this tour by yourself. It is more fun to dance with a partner.

Travel trip: Schedule in advance and make sure to bring a friend with you. On any night tour wear long pants to avoid getting mosquito bites.

16. ARDASTRA GARDENS, ZOO AND CONSERVATION CENTER IS THE BAHAMIAN VERSION OF A ZOO AND BOTANICAL GARDEN

I often hear it pronounced 'ad astra' like the 2019 space movie featuring Brad Pitt. You will see pink flamingo performing, sloths, birds, and wildlife. If that's not reason enough to visit I don't know what is.

Travel tip: They offer group discounts. You can schedule a private tour. You can get married there. You can schedule to have a private dinner there. Check with your hotel if they offer a discount for Ardastra Gardens. You can also check out their website or call ahead for additional information.

17. FEEDING NEEDS OF YOUR INFANTS

Most Bahamian grocery stores and pharmacies carry baby formulas or products; however, if you are brand conscious or if your baby has special needs, make sure you bring enough baby supplies to cover the length of your vacation.

Travel tip: Your baby is entitled to their luggage allowance, so stock up on everything you think you might need. Many hotels provide cribs and rental car seats can be obtained from car rental companies.

18. CLOTHING NEEDS FOR YOUR CHILDREN

Packing extra swimsuits are a must. Consider investing in water-resistant shoes or quality flip flops. Pick light colors from their wardrobe because light colors reflect the sunlight. Pack extra comfy socks.

Travel tip: Always do laundry as a group. Bring a small detergent bottle with you for laundry. Buy detergent from a local shop rather than the hotel to avoid paying a ridiculous surcharge.

19. CLOTHING NEEDS FOR YOURSELF

Packing extra swimsuits are a must. Consider investing in water-resistant shoes or quality flip flops. Bring light color clothing. Wear neutral tones that can be mixed and matched to create a new look. Pack a formal outfit if you have space. Bring your favorite cozy sweater or socks so you snuggle in your covers at night or take a night stroll on the beach comfortably.

Travel tip: You can rent formal outfits from some Bahamian clothing stores.

20. THE BAHAMAS IS AN ENVIRONMENTALLY FRIENDLY COUNTRY

The Bahamas has a ban on single-use plastics. Be prepared to expect cardboard straws, reusable utensils, and paper cups. Bring your reusable grocery bag with you so you can avoid paying a dollar for a single-use plastic bag. Local vendors are encouraged not to provide plastic bags to tourists. Many convenience and grocery stores do not provide plastic bags or reusable bags to purchase. Respect the country's move towards helping the environment and invest in a reusable grocery bag so you can shop without worrying about how to carry the items.

Travel tip: You can double your reusable grocery bag as your laundry bag during your stay, just make sure to wash it. You can buy reusable grocery bags at The Straw Market or in gift shops.

21. LEAVE NO TRACE (TRASH OR MARKINGS)

Bahamian beaches are cleaned several times a year; however, make sure to discard your trash in garbage cans to keep beaches safe and clean for everyone. It takes a lot of work to keep the beaches clean. The pristine state you will find the beaches in is usually the result of citizens discarding their waste appropriately and participating in a community beach clean-up when there's a build-up of trash.

22. HOW TO SEE THE WHOLE ISLAND

Do you want to see the island but save on taxis fare? You can take any bus and travel like a local. You can ride on a bus in Downtown.

All bus route typically takes an hour to circulate. The bus fare would be posted near the bus driver. The fare price for an adult is 1 dollar and 25 cents. The fare price for a child is usually 1 dollar.

Unfortunately, the country currently does not have a bus tracking app. However, you will find that the bus drivers are always willing to help tourists navigate through the system. You can use the bus system to get to supermarkets, dog-friendly parks, malls, art galleries, and local movie cinemas.

The number 15 bus will take you the Mall at Marathon, movie cinemas and supermarkets. You can catch this bus in Downtown.

Travel tip: If you are planning on riding the bus between lunch time (11:30am-1pm), before boarding make sure to ask the bus driver if he can drop you back. Yell 'bus stop' or 'stop' when you want the bus to drop you off immediately at a location you are about to approach. The Bahamas has distinctive bus stops along the bus route; however, you can just shout 'bus stop' and the driver will safely stop the bus for you to get off. If you want to stop an approaching bus in the distance to ride on it, you must stretch your arm out and flag them down to catch their attention.

23. CHARTER A BOAT OR YACHT FOR FISHING OR SAILING

The Bahamas is a great fishing and sailing location. You will have to hire a charter company to take you fishing or sailing. You can use fishing traps to get spiny lobster (crawfish) and conch. Just make sure to read up on the country's daily fishing allowance, it changes yearly. Fishing allowance is the weight of seafood you can legally take from the country's waters. The charter company provides a weight scale.

24. ARE ALL BEACHES FOR THE PUBLIC

By law technically all beachfront is public to the water but there are gated communities that restrict access to their private beaches. There's no distinguishable difference between the two. There are many beaches both on Nassau and on Paradise Island that offer different attractions. I prefer public beaches because there is safety in numbers, public restrooms, local beach eatery, and lively background music.

Travel tip: If you do not want to be bothered by local vendors selling their handmade products, you can simply tell them that you do not carry cash. Or you can be direct and politely thank them but say that you're not interest and are trying to enjoy time alone/with your family.

25. YOU CAN TRAVEL TO THE OUT ISLANDS/FAMILY ISLANDS

The Bahamas is an archipelago of around 700 islands and cays. The principal islands include

Abaco, Acklins, Andros, Berry Islands, Bimini, Cat Island, Crooked Island, Eleuthera, Exuma, Grand Bahama, Harbour Island, Inagua, Long Island, Mayaguana, New Providence (where the capital, Nassau, is located), Ragged Island, Rum Cay, San Salvador and Spanish Wells.

Many people do not consider traveling to the outer islands (other principal islands). Locals refer to the outer islands as 'family islands.' You can take a boat to a few locations, just be mindful that sail times can be affected by many different factors. The boat ride depending on your destination would be 3 to 4 hours. You will have access to the lower and upper deck. The boats have glass paneling, so you will be able to see ocean life like it is an underwater submarine ride. Along the boat ride, you will see fishes, turtles, and coral reefs ecosystem.

If you are an introvert and you want a noise-free vacation, I would highly recommend vacationing on the outer islands rather than the capital. From experience, I can say that the best reading I've done is on a beach in Eleuthera. It is guaranteed to have low occupancy year-round due to the lack of tourist marketing. The outer islands also offer similar water-based activities like the capital. The outer island is popular among the elderly and newlyweds. Some popular outer islands with highly rated hotels are Exuma, Freeport, Eleuthera, and Harbor Island.

Travel tip: If you are traveling with kids, make sure to pack games and keep a vigilant watch over them. You can ask your hotel if they'd recommend a local babysitter. Food is more expensive than the capital. There isn't a baggage allowance for the boat ride so, you can stock up on goodies at the capital before traveling to your destination.

26. MOST SURPRISING ROCK SHORE

Visitors are pleasantly greeted by a wide variety of mollusks, starfish, and sea urchins closer to the shoreline in between the crevices of the rocky shoreline. Please do not touch or remove the wildlife you will encounter. It is better to observe rather than interfere with this delicate eco-system.

27. FOOD PRICES AND VAT

The Bahamas must import products and goods. You might find the prices of items to more expensive compared to your home country. Value Added Tax (VAT) is currently 12% on every item except for bread and basket items. You can see the VAT excluded list which is updated yearly on the Bahamian government website.

28. ROSE ISLAND DAY TRIP

You can book this trip on TripAdvisor. The tour is described as, "combines a boat cruise, snorkeling excursion, and private beach—allowing you to experience multiple island highlights in one day." There will be stingrays and the occasional stray dolphin near the island. You can buy lunch at the island's café. There are hot and cold showers available on site.

Travel tip: The luggage compartment for the tour boat is smaller compared to other boats.

You just need a gym bag, duffle bag, or knapsack. Be mindful of what you pack. Make sure to pack a change of clothes, towel, and toiletries.

29. WATERPROOF CAMERA

Invest in a good quality water-proof camera to capture your water adventures. You will be able to bring the camera without worrying about water damage while you swim with the dolphins, scuba drive, or canoe.

Travel-tip: If you are looking for a cheaper option, you can buy a Kodak or Fuji disposable water camera for your trip. Vendors on Amazon sells these individually and in packs. If you do buy it, make sure to buy at least two. You can get your disposable camera photos developed in Bahamian photo studios.

30. BAHAMAS KAYAKING AND WATER SPORTS PACKAGE AT JUNKANOO BEACH

You can book them through TripAdvisor. For 2020, the posted price is $30 per person. This is the perfect water adventure for those who love thrills and excitement. You can get access to snorkel gear, kayaks, Banana boats, paddleboards, inflatables, and the water trampoline. They also hourly rent out beach sporting gear like soccer and volleyballs. You can use their services for up to six hours at a time. The number of activities to do are endless considering the time frame and it is affordable too. A huge plus is that most of the water activities are kids friendly.

31. NASSAU FOOD TASTING AND CULTURAL WALKING TOUR

This is hands down the best food tour to take if you want to try all the classic Bahamian food items like conch fritters, Bahamian mac 'n' cheese, and island specialty cocktails. The group tour is intimate allowing only 12 people. This is a great tour for solo travelers to take. You will learn interesting facts like the Bahamas was the landing site for Christopher Columbus.

Travel trip: Make sure to book this in advance if you have a large group.

32. NASSAU SUBMARINE ADVENTURE

This underwater adventure is curated by 'Stuart Cove Dive Bahamas'. It is perfect for swimmers and non-swimmers alike. You will be placed in a bubble suit. If you tie your hair up, it will not get wet. A huge plus is the complimentary hotel pickup and drop-off.

Travel trip: You must be waiting at the appointed hour. If you are not at the agreed meeting location, the bus will leave without you and you will not be refunded.

33. EXUMA ADVENTURES

Exuma Powerboat Adventure-Allen Cay Edition

This is an all-day adventure. You will be placed on a powerboat headed to a Cay in Eleuthera, Allen's Cay. There you will feed iguanas, stingrays, and sharks. You will have the opportunity to snorkel and explore the Cay. The food and drinks are included. There are showers located on site. A huge plus is the complimentary hotel pickup and drop-off.

Travel tip: Pack a book, headphones, and music with you. Create a vacation playlist that requires no Wi-Fi or data to load and be available, which you can refer to when you need an extra level of auditory comfort. There are lounge chairs and benches for your convenience. Bring a pair of long pants to protect your legs from mosquitoes.

Exuma Powerboat Adventure-Swimming Pig Edition

This is an all-day adventure. You will be placed on a powerboat headed to the Exuma Cays. There you will feed iguanas, sharks, and pigs. You will be offered refreshments on the boat and lunch is provided. You will have the opportunity to relax on a secluded beach.

Travel tip: Pack a book, headphones, and music with you. There are lounge chairs and benches for your convenience. Bring a pair of long pants to protect your legs from mosquitoes.

34. ATLANTIS (PARADISE ISLAND, NEW PROVIDENCE, BAHAMAS)

Things to do

The Atlantis resort is located on Paradise Island. Seeing the Atlantis resort for the first time literally takes one's breath away. One of the highlights that should be on everyone's bucket list is the open-air Marine Habitat. There's 11 million gallons of water and features different species of Lionfish, piranhas, jellyfish, groups, Moray Eels, Caribbean sharks, giant manta rays, and smaller 'Jewel Habitats' are home to multi-colored tropical fish. You can through a clear acrylic tunnel submerged in a lagoon filled with amazing marine life.

There's the 'Blue Lagoon Dolphin Swim' experience by Dolphin Encounters located on

Paradise Island where you'll get the opportunity swim, dance, hug, and learn about the dolphins habitat. There's also the 'Sea Lion Encounter' ad 'Stingray Encounter' experiences done by Dolphin Encounters. There are mandatory life jackets provided. The activity is great for swimmers and non-swimmers alike. You can go on a 'Segway Tour of Blue Lagoon Island'

You can go on a 'Shark Dive Adventure' done by Stuart Cove Bahamas. You will be able to see as many as 30 5-6ft Caribbean Reef Sharks. Your tour guide will point out the different fishes in the area like groups, snappers, nurse sharks, and baby sharks. You can book a private sunset cruise by ReeFun Adventures Tours.

Waterpark

The resort has the biggest water theme park in the Caribbean. There are high pressure water slides, river ride, wave surges, mile long water slide, hot tubs, and endless swimming pools. Make sure to watch the YouTube promotional videos to be sure of what to expect. Atlantis also has promotional videos on their website. Some cruise ship passengers choose to spend their time in Nassau at the Waterpark.

35. DIVERS AND SNORKELERS PARADISE

The Bahamas is known as the Divers and Snorkelers Paradise. There are many underwater caves to explore. You can book a guided scuba diving tour with The Bahamas Underground. Thunder ball Grotto is an underwater cave that was featured in two James Bond movies. If you are not an experienced swimmer and diver I would recommend this location. You can schedule to go when there's a low tide.

You can explore the deepest blue hole in The Bahamas, Dean's Blue Hole. Dean's Blue Hole is located in Long Island and is the world's second deepest, after the Dragon Hole in the South China Sea, with a depth of 202 meters (663 ft). Dean's Blue Hole is the home to annual free five championship known as 'Vertical Blue International Freediving Competition'. You might have seen the competition on television.

Travel tip: Coordinate with the tour guide which day would be perfect for a swim. You will need to rent professional scuba diving gear for cave exploration.

36. LUCAYAN NATIONAL PARK (GRAND BAHAMA ISLAND, BAHAMAS)

This park is a visually stunning representation of immaculate beauty. The beaches are beautiful with crystal clear waters, stunning sunsets, and breathtaking starry nights. You can explore the different caves there. You will learn about the mangrove ecosystem as well as many of the protected wildlife in the area.

Travel tip: Depending on when you want to go to Grand Bahama, taking a ferry/boat ride might be a cheaper option compared to taking a plane.

37. BAHAMAS OCEAN SAFARIS (ELEUTHERA ISLAND)

Spanish Wells, Eleuthera, is known for their crawfish industry. You can schedule a day trip there. The guide will take you on an historical and visual tour in the waters. The coral reef there is blooming with color and life. You might be able to see birds like the heron, crane, egret, and even some species of ducks.

Travel tip: Bring your waterproof camera with you to capture the beautiful oceanic life.

38. BRINGING YOUR BELOVED PET

It would be cost effective if you found a pet sitter in your home country rather than bringing your pet. The Bahamian government requires paperwork signed off by a registered vet. You can view the requirements on the Ministry of Agriculture website. In addition to submitting your pet's documents, you must pay for a pet permit during the length of your stay. All the forms can be found on the Ministry's website and you can submit them online.

The Bahamas must import products and goods. You might find the prices of your pet's essential items to be more expensive compared to your home country. Most grocery stores do sell pet food, but the brands selection is limited. If your pet has special needs and require a specific brand of food,

I recommend bringing enough to cover the length of your stay.

The Bahamian sunny weather and humidity can become dangerous for your pet if they are not well hydrated. Make sure that your pet water dish is always full. If your pet loves swimming, keep a watch on them when they are swimming in the ocean.

Travel tip: Many of the hotels in Nassau are not pet friendly. The hotels that are pet friendly have extra cleaning fees and you will have to put more money down on a deposit. If you plan on bringing your pet, I highly recommend getting a pet friendly Airbnb with washer and dryer units.

39. DATA ROAMING

There are two cell phone companies in the Bahamas, BTC and ALIV. Both companies have booths in the airport. I highly recommend you getting your luggage first, then try locating a booth. You can use your phone for anything involving the internet when you enroll in a Data Roaming Plan. The sign-up process only takes twenty minutes.

Travel tip: You might not need a Data Roaming Plan if you are planning on sticking to tours, tourist activities, and lodging in the hotel. Most tourist locations and restaurants offer free Wi-Fi.

40. BAHA-MAR RESORT

The Baha-Mar Resort is a resort complex in Nassau, Bahamas. It currently has three hotels Grand Hyatt, SLS Baha Mar, and the Rosewood. It is the newest resort in the Bahamas.

The resort has an incredible casino, multiple dining options, swim-up bar, outdoor pools, easy access to the beach, fitness club, nightclub, spa with sauna, steam rooms, kids' club, movie theater and other amenities. The hotel claims to be wheelchair accessible throughout the resort. The hotel is pet-friendly, allowing your pets to join you in the pool and at some select restaurants. Some designer brand boutiques on site are Rolex, Bulgari, and Tiffany.

41. SOLO TRAVELLING TIPS

Rent a car or use the bus system

All the tours are solo traveler friendly, unless otherwise states in the description

Make sure to stick to groups when participating in water activities

Make sure to carry an ID with you

If you have allergies or special needs make sure you have it on a medical bracelet

Share and update your digital itinerary regularly with your family and friends

Make sure you sign up for a Data Roaming Plan

Pack a selfie stick or camera extension

Don't get too drunk in public. Always only drink one to two glasses. If you want to drink more always choose to buy your liquor to carry back to your room.

42. SOUVENIRS TO BRING HOME

You should check out the Straw Market and pick smaller items to carry back with you for your family and friends. You can find suitcase space friendly shot glasses, magnets, pins, hair accessories, cutlery, or even bracelets.

43. GOLF SCENE

The Bahamas is known for hosting international Golf Tournaments. Recently the Bahamas hosted the 2019 Hero World Challenge at the Albany Resort. The golf courses are where some celebrities are known to practice their skills on their offseason. You might be able to catch a glimpse of Tiger Woods.

Travel tip: Golf Instructors are in-demand contract employees. Be sure to call ahead to the Golf Club and schedule an appointment with an instructor.

44. MONEY SAVING HACKS

You should always make sure that your money makes money especially when it comes to saving up for a vacation. There are so many ways to earn interest on your extra funds. If you tend to use your card more than physical cash, you can consider opening a reward checking account. You'll have to view your bank's program or different banks rewards programs to compare to come to the best decision for yourself and for your wallet.

You can also open a saving account with a bank that offer a high APY (annual percentage yield). Make sure to investigate the APY that your company or community saving account offers depending on where you work and live. Always set up automatic withdrawal to be dated on the date prior to receiving your paycheck. This will lessen the likelihood that you'll end up spending that money.

If you have high level of self-control, you can consider having a 'no buy year', establish your 'no buy year' rules, and budget your essential expenses until you have enough money saved up for your vacation.

Depending on where you live, you can rent out your car, guesthouse, or professional equipment for extra cash. You can use your professional talents on weekends like working on Fiverr and Upwork or by doing minimum wage jobs like dog walking, pet sitting, baby-sitting, etc.

How to Stay on Budget when in The Bahamas:

If you are tech savvy, you can create a budget tracking sheet on Google Sheets. If you prefer to jot down your spending, bring a small notebook with you to track down all card and cash expenses to make sure you are sticking with your budget.

How Much to Tip in The Bahamas:

Some visitors do not realize that many Bahamian restaurants automatically add gratuity to the bill. If gratuity is not included, be sure to tip your server or bartender 15-20% of your bill's total.

Travel tip: You should not tip your taxi drivers. You should not tip the hotel's shuttle bus driver.

45. BEST PLACES TO GO SHOPPING

The shops located in Downtown and the stores in the Mall of Marathon are two great locations to shop for apparel and accessories. There are some designers' boutiques in hotels like Atlantis and Bahamar.

For groceries, I recommend chain stores like Super Value, City Market, and Solomon's Fresh Market. You are most likely to find food brands you are familiar with.

Travel tip: Bahamas has a ban on single-use plastics. You should always bring your re-useable bags with you.

46. WHAT IS CONCH?

Conch is pounced "konk". This is a meat from a pink-lipped and spiral-shelled Queen Conch (large sea snail). The snail is native to the coasts of the Bahamas. Due to other countries overfishing their conch population, The Bahamas is one of the few countries where large populations exist. The Conch population and harvesting is being closely monitored so it will remain a strong economic source for years to come. The nationwide campaign "Conchseration" is aimed at protecting the Queen Conch from the further stock decline through development and awareness of sustainable fishing practices.

It is commonly eaten fresh (raw) or cooked. Conch does not have a fishy smell. It tastes salty, you get flavor profiles of both crab and clams. Conch is relatively cheap to buy at the docks. All Bahamian restaurants sell dishes featuring it in fritters, cracked conch burgers, chowders, and stew.

The three popular conch dishes in The Bahamas are conch fritters, cracked conch, and conch salad. Conch Salad ingredients are raw conch, tomato, cucumber, onions, sweet pepper, chiles, salt, and the citrus juices like lime or orange. Conch fritters are small fried dough balls with conch in them. The batter is like the American hush puppy batter, but it has onion, sweet peppers, conch and tomatoes in it. Conch fritters is served with a dipping sauce made up of goat pepper, dried spices, hot sauce, and mayo. Cracked conch is pounded and breaded like fried chicken using buttermilk, eggs, and breadcrumbs before frying until crispy golden brown.

Travel tip: The best conch salad on the Island is at the Potter's Cay Dock. The Potter's Cay is a farmer's market offering freshly caught seafood, local fruits and vegetables, and smaller local seafood booths. Potter's Cay Dock is a great place to shop for fish, crawfish, lobster, conch, and crabs. Potter's Cay Dock vendors only accept cash.

47. LIST OF BAHAMIAN FOOD, DRINK AND HISTORICAL SITES TO SEE

Guava Duff: Dessert made up of guavas and pastry dough. It is served with rum custard.

Daiquiri: Dessert. See **tip #9.**

Rum Cake: Dessert. See **tip #12.**

Macaroni N' Cheese: Bahamian Mac N' Cheese is baked, and the recipe differs depending on where you dine. The dish's main ingredients are cheddar cheese, eggs, milk, and butter. It might include either sweet pepper, onion, bacon, or ham.

Pigeon Peas N' Rice: This savory side dish is made up of pigeon peas, brown/white rice, celery, tomatoes, thyme, tomato pasta, bacon/pork, goat pepper, and onions.

Crab N' Rice: This side dish is mistaken as Crab Fried Rice. The crab population in the Bahamas is thriving. Bahamian Land Crabs are added to 'Pigeon Peas N' Rice' during the cooking process. This rice is not fried.

Conch Salad: See **tip #46.**

Conch Fritters: See **tip #46.**

Cracked Conch: See **tip #46.**

Spiny Lobsters (aka Rock Lobsters): This is commonly referred to as crawfish in the Bahamas. You can find this on any seafood restaurant menu. The recipe and preparation of crawfish differs in each restaurant.

Souse (famous Bahamian stew/soup) & Johnnycake: Pronounced as 'sowse'. This soup is commonly eaten as a breakfast item. The soup ingredients are onions, lime juice, celery, sweet peppers, potatoes, carrots, bay leaves, and your choice of meat-chicken, sheep's tongue, pork, oxtail, or pig's feet. It is served with a lime wedge on the side and either johnnycake or home-made bread. Johnnycake is pan-cooked bread usually served with souse. Johnnycake is made of milk, butter, flour, and sugar.

Stew Fish: Locals call it 'Boiled Fish'. Bahamian chefs usually use either grouper or snapper as their fish of choice for this dish. The fish is simmered with onions, potatoes, carrots, thyme, tomato paste, pepper, and seasonings. It is served with a lime wedge on the side and either johnnycake, grits, or home-made bread.

Switcha: This is a popular non-alcoholic Bahamian lemon-lime flavored lemonade found in all restaurants and stores.

Goombay Punch: See **tip #13.**

Goombay Smash: See **tip #13.**

Beers: See **tip #10**

John Watling's Distillery: The tour takes 20-30 minutes depending on your guide. You can taste the drinks prepared by the staff and buy rum from their gift shop.

Yellow Bird: This is a cocktail of rum and citrus fruits.

Painkiller: This is a cocktail includes rum, orange juice, pineapple juice, coconut cream, and nutmeg.

Hibiscus Margarita: This cocktail of lime juice, agave nectar, tequila, and hibiscus syrup/hibiscus tea.

Sky Juice (aka Gully Wash or Gully Wow): This cocktail includes coconut water, sweetened condensed milk, coconut pulp, and gin. It is a powerful sweet cocktail

Bahama Mama: It is one of the most requested rum drinks at resorts. You will find a pineapple or orange wedge on the rim. It contains both light and dark rum, lemon juice, pineapple juice, coffee-flavored liquor, and cherries.

Bahama Punch: Rum and hand-made fruit cocktail with pineapple juice, coconut rum, orange juice, and Campari bitters.

Bahama Bay Breeze: This drink has vodka, cranberry juice, and pineapple juice.

Pirates of Nassau: The museum is in Downtown. You will see wax figurines, historic antiques, and learn of the pirate history in the Bahamas. You are encouraged to take photos anywhere. This museum is a fun activity for kids. Once you are in downtown, the path to the museum is walk friendly.

Fort: You honestly do not need to book a tour to see any of the forts. The forts are located relatively close to Downtown. To my knowledge, there are no streetlamps near the forts; so, you should plan to go there during the day. I would recommend Fort Charlotte. The path is walk friendly and Fort Charlotte is the closest to Arawak Cay. You can visit the Fort Charlotte first then head over to Arawak Cay for lunch and try the local dishes.

Queen's Staircase & Fort Fincastle: The Queen's Staircase is referred to the 66 steps. It is a major landmark on most tours. The staircase was made by slaves in the 1790s and it was carved out of limestones rocks. It is located nearest to the Fort Fincastle. To get the best picture of this site I would suggest trying to go there mid-afternoon or early morning when there's less crowds and the sun's not shining too brightly. You do not need to pay admissions or need a tour guide to access this site.

Cloisters (Paradise Island): I find that many tourists are unaware of this beautiful site. This is the old European ruins and it's surrounded by a beautiful garden in the Spring. The ruins are on the site owned by the Ocean Club. The Ocean Club is a luxury hotel. The Cloisters is open to the public free of charge 24/7. However, the site is popular for destination weddings and private events so sometimes security will not permit entry to the grounds.

Doongalik Studios: You'll have to book a taxi ride there. If you are in the area of Montagu Beach, you can walk there. You can see locally made paintings, crafts, and pottery. There are large scale original sculptures outside for taking photos. The caretakers will be happy to give you a tour and tell you of the stories or inspiration behind each piece.

Travel tip: You can ask the bartender to make any of the Bahamian cocktails into a mocktail (non-alcoholic).

48. LIST OF ESSENTIAL ITEMS

Passport/Visa

Driver's License

Medical or vaccination record

Print your Digital Confirmations, like your Hotel, Car, or Tour Confirmations

Prescription medication that is labelled correctly

Print your Digital Tickets, like your Music Festival, Celebrity Shows, or to Movie Tickets

Credit cards and Cash

Emergency Money if you can't find an ATM

Reusable Bags

Sunscreen/Sunblock

Hat

Water-proof camera

Electric power bank

Download useful apps

Windbreaker/Light Sweater

Sunglasses

Backpack/Gym bag

Swimsuit

Loose fitting pants

Insect Repellent

49. MAKE A BAHAMAS BUCKET LIST

Make a personalized bucket list that breaks down your goals, wanting experiences, and travel itinerary during your vacation. Writing down your vacation goals will help you stay on track and it ensures that you are experiencing all that the Island offers.

50. MAKE THE MOST OF YOUR TRIP

Try your best to schedule your tours while you are in your home country. Worst case scenario is that you book your dream vacation to the Bahamas and most of the tours are already booked. The best-case scenario is that you plan and made the most of your vacation time.

Don't over schedule your time. Try to have a cool down time between each booking so you won't be overwhelmed trying to rush over to the next scheduled appointment. Use your cool down periods to do activities that make you genuinely happy like

73

shopping, trying new cuisine, drinking, swimming, or reading by the poolside.

Let your employer and family know that you might be offline for most of your trip. Disconnecting from the internet is the most rewarding opportunity on any vacation because it is not possible in everyday life. You will be able to take everything and preserve memories of your vacation for years to come.

"We travel because we need to, because distance and difference are the secret tonic of creativity. When we get home, home is still the same. But something in our mind has been changed, and that changes everything." –Jonah Lehrer.

AFTERWORD

I hope you've found this book useful. I know sometimes people find traveling to a new country a little bit daunting. My whole goal was to make it simple and to the point without having you feeling overwhelmed with information. Remember to do your own research because tours, prices, and availability might change. Please check out the other books in the GREATER THAN A TOURIST series and leave a review on the book.

TRIVIA

1) Who owns The Bahamas?

2) Bahamas is known to be the landing site for who?

3) How much time does a bus take to lap around their route?

4) Where is the deepest blue hole?

5) What are the two main currencies used in The Bahamas?

6) What two conch-based dishes do locals usually like to eat?

7) What language is mainly spoken in the Bahamas?

8) What is the nationwide campaign dedicated to protecting the Queen Conch?

9) Name the hurricane that destroyed Abaco in 2019.

10) Does it snow in the Bahamas?

ANSWERS

1) Bahamas is an independent country

2) Christopher Columbus

3) 1 hour (without traffic jams)

4) In the Bahamas: Dean's Blue Hole on Long Island is the deepest blue hole in The Bahamas

5) The Bahamian dollar (BSD) and the American dollar (USD)

6) Conch salad and conch fritters

7) English

8) Conchservation

9) Hurricane Dorian

10) No. (It did snow once on Freeport, Bahamas in the past but it has not since then)

PACKING AND PLANNING TIPS

A Week before Leaving

- Arrange for someone to take care of pets and water plants.

- Email and Print important Documents.

- Get Visa and vaccines if needed.

- Check for travel warnings.

- Stop mail and newspaper.

- Notify Credit Card companies where you are going.

- Passports and photo identification is up to date.

- Pay bills.

- Copy important items and download travel Apps.

- Start collecting small bills for tips.

- Have post office hold mail while you are away.

- Check weather for the week.

- Car inspected, oil is changed, and tires have the correct pressure.

- Check airline luggage restrictions.

- Download Apps needed for your trip.

Right Before Leaving

- Contact bank and credit cards to tell them your location.

- Clean out refrigerator.

- Empty garbage cans.

- Lock windows.

- Make sure you have the proper identification with you.

- Bring cash for tips.

- Remember travel documents.

- Lock door behind you.

- Remember wallet.

- Unplug items in house and pack chargers.

- Change your thermostat settings.

- Charge electronics, and prepare camera memory cards.

READ OTHER
GREATER THAN A TOURIST
BOOKS

Greater Than a Tourist- Geneva Switzerland: 50 Travel Tips from a Local by Amalia Kartika

Greater Than a Tourist- St. Croix US Birgin Islands USA: 50 Travel Tips from a Local by Tracy Birdsall

Greater Than a Tourist- San Juan Puerto Rico: 50 Travel Tips from a Local by Melissa Tait

Greater Than a Tourist – Lake George Area New York USA: 50 Travel Tips from a Local by Janine Hirschklau

Greater Than a Tourist – Monterey California United States: 50 Travel Tips from a Local by Katie Begley

Greater Than a Tourist – Chanai Crete Greece: 50 Travel Tips from a Local by Dimitra Papagrigoraki

Greater Than a Tourist – The Garden Route Western Cape Province South Africa: 50 Travel Tips from a Local by Li-Anne McGregor van Aardt

Greater Than a Tourist – Sevilla Andalusia Spain: 50 Travel Tips from a Local by Gabi Gazon

Children's Book: *Charlie the Cavalier Travels the World* by Lisa Rusczyk Ed. D.

> TOURIST

Follow us on Instagram for beautiful travel images:
http://Instagram.com/GreaterThanATourist

Follow *Greater Than a Tourist* on Amazon.
>Tourist Podcast
>T Website
>T Youtube
>T Facebook
>T Goodreads
>T Amazon
>T Mailing List
>T Pinterest
>T Instagram
>T Twitter
>T SoundCloud
>T LinkedIn
>T Map

> TOURIST

At *Greater Than a Tourist*, we love to share travel tips with you. How did we do? What guidance do you have for how we can give you better advice for your next trip? Please send your feedback to GreaterThanaTourist@gmail.com as we continue to improve the series. We appreciate your constructive feedback. Thank you.

METRIC CONVERSIONS

TEMPERATURE

110° F — — 40° C
100° F —
90° F — — 30° C
80° F —
70° F — — 20° C
60° F —
50° F — — 10° C
40° F —
32° F — — 0° C
20° F —
10° F — — -10° C
0° F — — -18° C
-10° F —
-20° F — — -30° C

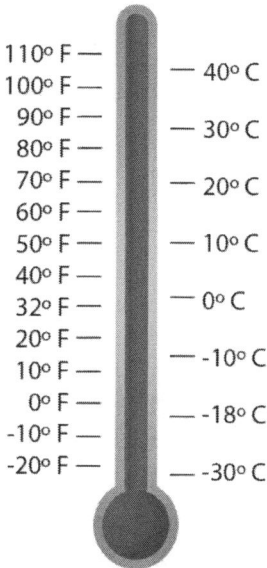

To convert F to C:
Subtract 32, and then multiply by 5/9 or .5555.

To Convert C to F:
Multiply by 1.8 and then add 32.

32F = 0C

LIQUID VOLUME

To Convert:.................Multiply by
U.S. Gallons to Liters................ 3.8
U.S. Liters to Gallons 26
Imperial Gallons to U.S. Gallons 1.2
Imperial Gallons to Liters....... 4.55
Liters to Imperial Gallons 22
1 Liter = .26 U.S. Gallon
1 U.S. Gallon = 3.8 Liters

DISTANCE

To convert ....Multiply by
Inches to Centimeters 2.54
Centimeters to Inches 39
Feet to Meters........................ .3
Meters to Feet 3.28
Yards to Meters 91
Meters to Yards 1.09
Miles to Kilometers 1.61
Kilometers to Miles............ .62
1 Mile = 1.6 km
1 km = .62 Miles

WEIGHT

1 Ounce = .28 Grams
1 Pound = .4555 Kilograms
1 Gram = .04 Ounce
1 Kilogram = 2.2 Pounds

TRAVEL QUESTIONS

- Do you bring presents home to family or friends after a vacation?

- Do you get motion sick?

- Do you have a favorite billboard?

- Do you know what to do if there is a flat tire?

- Do you like a sun roof open?

- Do you like to eat in the car?

- Do you like to wear sun glasses in the car?

- Do you like toppings on your ice cream?

- Do you use public bathrooms?

- Did you bring a cell phone and does it have power?

- Do you have a form of identification with you?

- Have you ever been pulled over by a cop?

- Have you ever given money to a stranger on a road trip?

- Have you ever taken a road trip with animals?

- Have you ever gone on a vacation alone?

- Have you ever run out of gas?

- If you could move to any place in the world, where would it be?

- If you could travel anywhere in the world, where would you travel?

- If you could travel in any vehicle, which one would it be?

- If you had three things to wish for from a magic genie, what would they be?

- If you have a driver's license, how many times did it take you to pass the test?

- What are you the most afraid of on vacation?

- What do you want to get away from the most when you are on vacation?

- What foods smell bad to you?

- What item do you bring on ever trip with you away from home?

- What makes you sleepy?

- What song would you love to hear on the radio when you're cruising on the highway?

- What travel job would you want the least?

- What will you miss most while you are away from home?

- What is something you always wanted to try?

- What is the best road side attraction that you ever saw?

- What is the farthest distance you ever biked?

- What is the farthest distance you ever walked?

- What is the weirdest thing you needed to buy while on vacation?

- What is your favorite candy?

- What is your favorite color car?

- What is your favorite family vacation?

- What is your favorite food?

- What is your favorite gas station drink or food?

- What is your favorite license plate design?

- What is your favorite restaurant?

- What is your favorite smell?

- What is your favorite song?

- What is your favorite sound that nature makes?

- What is your favorite thing to bring home from a vacation?

- What is your favorite vacation with friends?

- What is your favorite way to relax?

- Where is the farthest place you ever traveled in a car?

- Where is the farthest place you ever went North, South, East and West?

- Where is your favorite place in the world?

- Who is your favorite singer?

- Who taught you how to drive?

- Who will you miss the most while you are away?

- Who if the first person you will contact when you get to your destination?

- Who brought you on your first vacation?

- Who likes to travel the most in your life?

- Would you rather be hot or cold?

- Would you rather drive above, below, or at the speed limited?

- Would you rather drive on a highway or a back road?

- Would you rather go on a train or a boat?

- Would you rather go to the beach or the woods?

TRAVEL BUCKET LIST

1.

2.

3.

4.

5.

6.

7.

8.

9.

10.

NOTES

Made in the USA
Middletown, DE
21 March 2022